KETO DIET FOR BEGINNERS

The Ultimate Keto Cookbook with Easy to Cook Ketogenic Diet Recipes for Rapid Weight Loss

SIMON BROCK

COPYRIGHT 2019 BY SIMON BROCK
ALL RIGHTS RESERVED

"you need to eat fat in order to burn fat."

—ERIC WESTMAN

CONTENT

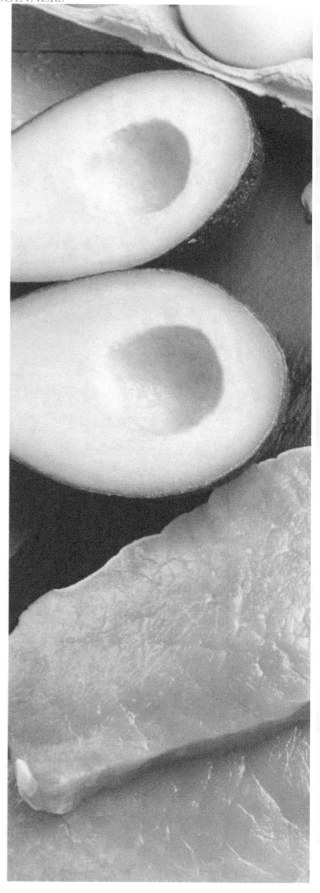

CONTENT

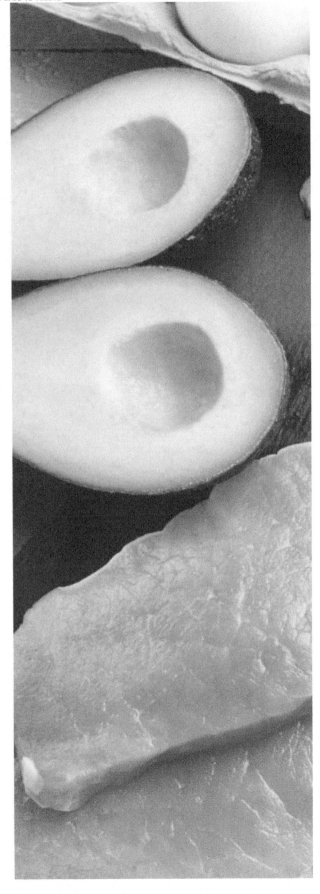

KETO DIET INTRODUCTION

A ketogenic diet is a high-fat, low-carb diet which will drastically reduce your daily carb intake and replace it with healthy fat. The reduction of carb helps the body to assume a state known as ketosis.

In this condition, the body becomes extremely efficient and burns fat for energy. It also helps to transform fat into ketones in the liver, which results in supplying energy to the brain.

With a ketogenic diet, one can experience huge reductions in insulin levels and blood sugar. The increased number of ketones includes a number of health benefits.

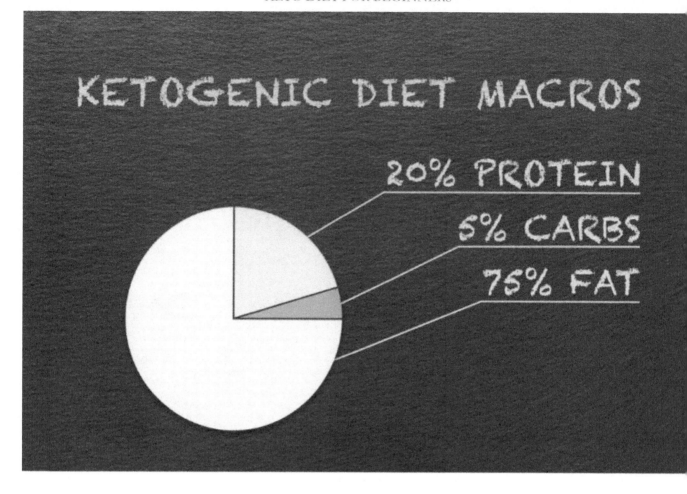

A number of versions of ketogenic diet are noted:

1. Standard ketogenic diet or SKD is a moderate-protein, low-carb, and high-fat diet, which contains 20% protein, 75% fat, and 5% carb.

2. Targeted ketogenic diet or TKD includes carbs around workouts.

3. Cyclical ketogenic diet or CKD allows you to have higher carb refeeds like 5 intense ketogenic days followed by 2 high-carb days.

4. High-protein ketogenic diet is almost like a standard ketogenic diet with the only exception of including more protein. The ratio stands as 60% fat, 5% carb, and 35% protein.

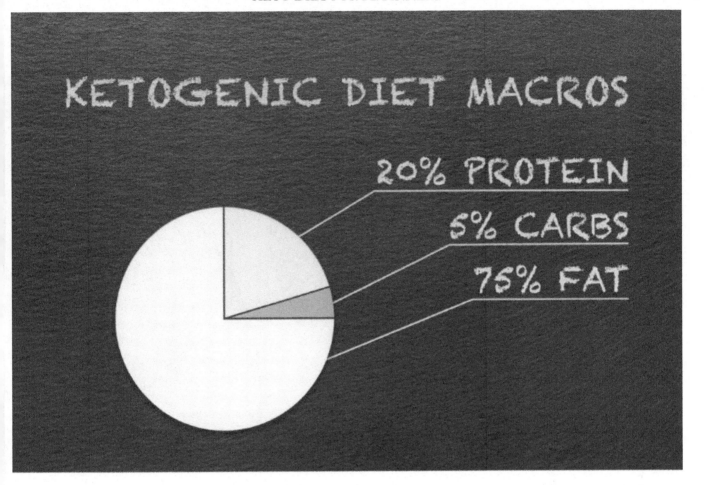

Cyclical and targeted ketogenic diets are more advanced and are normally given to athletes and bodybuilders.

A ketogenic diet is one of the effective ways to lose weight and decrease factors for disease such as high pressure and high blood sugar. It has been found out that people in a ketogenic diet have lost 2.2 times more weight than those in a calorie-restricted low-fat diet.

Apart from regular diseases, the ketogenic diet has also proved to be beneficial for several types of cancer and slow the growth of tumor. It has also shown remarkable progress in people suffering from Alzheimer's disease; the diet has slowed the progress of the disease.

FOOD ITEMS TO AVOID

Any food item that is high in carbs should be avoided in a ketogenic diet.

Check out the top 10 foods that should be avoided:

1. **Starches or grains**: wheat-based products such as cereal, pasta, or rice.

2. **Sugary items**: smoothies, cake, fruit juices, soda, candy, and ice cream.

3. **Beans or legumes**: kidney beans, chickpeas, lentils, and peas.

4. **Fruit**: all fruits except maybe a handful of strawberries.

5. **Tubers and root vegetables**: sweet potatoes, carrots, potatoes, and parsnips.

6. **Some sauces or condiments**: often these items contain unhealthy fat or sugar.

7. **Diet products**: these are highly processed and are high in carbs.

8. **Alcohol**: the carb content in alcohol will disrupt your ketosis.

9. **Unhealthy fats**: forgo processed vegetable oils.

10. **Sugar-free diet food items**

FOOD ITEMS TO TAKE

The majority of your meals should be based on these food items:

1. **Fatty fish**: trout, salmon, mackerel, and tuna.

2. **Meat**: sausage, red meat, ham, steak, turkey, bacon, and chicken.

3. **Butter and cream**: always look for grass-fed items.

4. **Eggs**: go for omega-3 whole eggs or pastured eggs.

5. **Healthy oils**: extra-virgin olive oil, avocado, and coconut oil.

6. **Cheese**: mainly unprocessed like goat, mozzarella, cheddar, blue, or cream.

7. **Seeds and nuts**: walnuts, chia, pumpkin, almonds, and flax seeds.

8. **Condiments**: salt, pepper, spices, and healthy herbs.

9. **Low-carb veggies**: mostly tomatoes, onions, green veggies, and peppers.

10. **Avocados**: freshly made guacamole or fresh avocados.

BREAKFAST RECIPES

AVOCADO BURGER

AVOCADO BURGER

GENERAL INFO

Serving Size: 1 Burger
Servings Per Recipe: 1
Calories: 211
Preparation Time: 15 Minutes
Cooking Time: 5 Minutes

INGREDIENTS

1 egg
1 ripe avocado
1 freshly sliced tomato
1 freshly sliced red onion
2 bacon rashers
1 tablespoon of paleo mayonnaise
Sea salt as required
1 lettuce leaf
Sesame seeds for garnishing

NUTRITION INFO

Carbohydrate—6g
Protein—84 g
Fat—121 g

AVOCADO BURGER

DIRECTIONS

1. On a cold frying pan, first put the bacon rashers; then, turn on the stove and start frying the bacon. Once the bacon starts to curl, you can simply flip it with a fork. You should continue to cook the bacon till it is crispy.

2. After removing the bacon, you can crack the eggs in the same pan. No need to put extra oil, as the bacon oil will be enough for the eggs as well. Cook the eggs till the white is set, but let the yolk remain runny.

3. Take the avocado and slice it in half widthwise. Use a spoon to scoop out the flesh and throw away the pit.

4. The hole of the avocado should be filled with paleo mayonnaise.

5. Now start layering it with lettuce, tomato, onion, and bacon and top it with the fried egg.

6. Sprinkle some sea salt over it and then top it with the other half of the avocado.

7. Put some sesame seeds over it and your healthy avocado bun is ready to be savored.

Recipe Notes

BLT SALAD

BLT SALAD - APT FOR BREAKFAST

GENERAL INFO

Serving Size: 1 Salad
Servings Per Recipe: 2 Yielding
Calories: 292
Preparation Time: 5 Minutes
Cooking Time: 10 Minutes

INGREDIENTS

1 teaspoon of red wine vinegar
3 cups of shredded lacinato kale
Kosher salt
2 teaspoons of extra-virgin olive oil
2 ounces of sliced avocado
2 large eggs
Black pepper as required
4 strips of cooked and chopped center-cut bacon
10 freshly halved grape tomatoes

NUTRITION INFO

Fat—18 g
Cholesterol—191 mg
Carbohydrate—9 g
Sodium—335.5 mg
Protein—17.5 g

BLT SALAD - APT FOR BREAKFAST

DIRECTIONS

1. Take a large salad bowl and put in the kale, vinegar, ¼ teaspoon of salt, and olive oil. Gently massage all the ingredients till the kale becomes soft.
2. Now put a pan on the stove and cook the egg as you desire; soft boiled eggs go really well with this BLT salad.
3. Now divide the kale in two bowls; top each of them with bacon, avocado, eggs, and tomato.
4. Sprinkle salt and pepper as required.
5. Dig into this bowl of healthy goodness and kick-start your morning.

Recipe Notes

BROCCOLI MUFFIN

BROCCOLI MUFFIN WITH A CHEESY TOUCH

GENERAL INFO

Serving Size: 1
Servings Per Recipe: 6
Calories: 374
Preparation Time: 5 Minutes
Cooking Time: 30 Minutes

INGREDIENTS

Mixing bowl
Muffin tin
2 large pasture-raised eggs
1 teaspoon of softened ghee and some extra ghee for greasing purpose
2 cups of almond flour
1 cup of unsweetened almond milk
1 cup of finely chopped broccoli florets
1 teaspoon of baking powder
2 teaspoons of nutritional yeast
½ teaspoon of sea salt

NUTRITION INFO

Fat—31.8 g
Cholesterol—174 mg
Carbohydrate—9.24 g
Sodium—467 mg
Protein—17.5 g

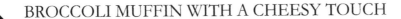

BROCCOLI MUFFIN WITH A CHEESY TOUCH

DIRECTIONS

1. First, you need to preheat the oven to 350°F. Take a large muffin tin and grease it with ghee.
2. In a large mixing bowl, gently stir all the ingredients. If you want, you can separately mix the dry and wet ingredients and then combine it in the large bowl.
3. Now take the muffin mixture and put them in muffin tins. You should bake the muffins for about half an hour. You will know that the muffins are ready when you insert a toothpick inside the muffin and it comes out clean.
4. You can also substitute the almond flour with coconut flour, but decrease the amount to half.
5. Your healthy muffins are ready to be enjoyed!

Recipe Notes

CAULIFLOWER FRITTERS

CAULIFLOWER FRITTERS SERVED HOT AND CRISPY

GENERAL INFO

Serving Size: 1
Servings Per Recipe: 6
Calories: 78
Preparation Time: 15 Minutes
Cooking Time: 10 Minutes

INGREDIENTS

Food processor
Large skillet
1–2 teaspoons of ghee
2 eggs
Large pot
Spatula
Mixing bowl
1 large head of cauliflower, which is broken into florets
2/3 cup of almond flour
½ teaspoon of sea salt
1 teaspoon of nutritional yeast
¼ teaspoon of black pepper
½ teaspoon of turmeric

NUTRITION INFO

Carbohydrate—3.2 g
Protein—5 g
Fat—7.1 g

CAULIFLOWER FRITTERS SERVED HOT AND CRISPY

DIRECTIONS

1. In a large pot filled with water, add the cauliflower and bring it to boil. It will take about 8 minutes to boil the entire cauliflower. Strain the water.

2. Now add the florets in a food processor and blend it until they are riced.

3. In a large mixing bowl, add the eggs, cauliflower, almond flour, turmeric, nutritional yeast, pepper, and salt. Give it a good stir so that they are mixed well. Flatten them and form patties.

4. Put a skillet on medium heat and heat the ghee. Scoop half the mixture which will amount to three fritters and cook them until they are golden brown on both sides. It will take about 3–4 minutes to cook the fritters.

5. Cook all the fritters and serve them hot with your favorite dip or sauce.

Recipe Notes

MEAT BAGELS

MEAT BAGELS

GENERAL INFO

Serving Size: 1
Servings Per Recipe: 6
Calories: 226
Preparation Time: 10 Minutes
Cooking Time: 30 Minutes

INGREDIENTS

1 teaspoon of bacon fat/grass-fed ghee/butter
1 ½ finely diced onions
2 pounds of ground pork
2 large eggs
1 teaspoon of paprika
2/3 cup of tomato sauce
1 teaspoon of salt
1 teaspoon of pepper

NUTRITION INFO

Fat—69 g
Cholesterol—94 mg
Carbohydrate—4.2 g
Sodium—298 mg
Protein—33 g

MEAT BAGELS

DIRECTIONS

1. First, you need to preheat the oven to 400° F. Take a baking dish and line it with parchment paper.
2. In a pan, take some cooking fat like butter or grass-fed ghee and sauté the onions at medium heat till they are translucent.
3. The onions should cool down before they are added to the meat.
4. Take a bowl and mix everything including the cooked onions. Give it a good mix so that all the spices get infused in the meat.
5. Now you should divide the meat into 6 portions. Roll one portion into a ball with your hands and create an indent in the middle. Flatten it slightly to make it look like a bagel.
6. Now put the bagel looking meat in the baking dish, and repeat this process with all the portions.
7. You should bake the meat for 40 minutes, so that the meat is fully cooked.
8. Let the meat bagels to cool down; slice the meat bagel and fill it with toppings like lettuce, tomato slices, and onions.
9. Enjoy this innovative meat bagel for breakfast.

Recipe Notes

KETO
PANCAKES

QUICK-FIX KETO PANCAKES

GENERAL INFO

Serving Size: 1
Servings Per Recipe: 10
Calories: 339
Preparation Time: 5 Minutes
Cooking Time: 15 Minutes

INGREDIENTS

4 ounces of softened cream cheese
½ cup of almond flour
1 teaspoon of lemon zest
Butter
4 large eggs

NUTRITION INFO

Fat—30 g
Potassium—145 mg
Carbohydrate—7 g
Cholesterol—207 mg
Protein—12 g

QUICK-FIX KETO PANCAKES

DIRECTIONS

1. Take a medium-size bowl and whisk almond flour, lemon zest, cream cheese, and eggs until you form a smooth batter.
2. Put a nonstick skillet on medium heat and melt 1 tablespoon of butter. Take 3 tablespoons of batter and cook them until they are golden. It will take about 2 minutes.
3. Flip the pancake and cook for another 2 minutes. Transfer it to a plate.
4. Enjoy the warm pancake with the toppings of your choice.
5. You can also serve them with the rest of the butter.

LUNCH
RECIPES

SHRIMP SALAD

AVOCADO SHRIMP SALAD

GENERAL INFO

Serving Size: 1
Servings Per Recipe: 2
Calories: 430
Preparation Time: 15 Minutes
Cooking Time: 5 Minutes

NUTRITION INFO

Fat—33 g
Sodium—1,250 mg
Potassium—600 mg
Cholesterol—143 mg
Carbohydrate—12.5 g
Protein—24 g

INGREDIENTS

1 freshly diced large avocado
1 drained and freshly diced beefsteak tomato
8 ounces of deveined and peeled shrimps, patted dry
2 tablespoons of melted salted butter
1/3 cup of crumbled feta cheese
1 tablespoon of freshly squeezed lemon juice
1/3 cup of freshly chopped parsley or cilantro
¼ teaspoon of salt
1 tablespoon of olive oil
¼ teaspoon of black pepper

AVOCADO SHRIMP SALAD

DIRECTIONS

1. Take a large bowl, put in the shrimp, and toss it in melted butter; the shrimp should be well coated with butter.
2. Put a pan on medium-high heat and add the shrimp in a single layer. Sear the shrimp for a minute or so until the shrimp starts to become pink in the edges. Flip the shrimp and cook them for another minute.
3. Transfer the shrimp to a plate after you are done with cooking. Allow the shrimp to cool down while you prepare the other ingredients.
4. In a large mixing bowl, add all the ingredients like the diced avocado, feta cheese, lemon juice, olive oil, diced tomato, cilantro, pepper, and salt. Give the ingredients a good toss.
5. Add the shrimp and mix it well. Serve this fresh salad. This is perfect for those days when you desire to have a light lunch.

Recipe Notes

GRILLED CHEESE

GRILLED CHEESE WITH A CRISPY ZUCCHINI CRUST

GENERAL INFO

Serving Size: 1
Servings Per Recipe: 4
Calories: 155
Preparation Time: 15 Minutes
Cooking Time: 20 Minutes

NUTRITION INFO

Fat—10 g
Carbohydrate—5 g
Protein—10 g

INGREDIENTS

For zucchini crust "bread" slices:
1 egg
1 teaspoon of dried oregano
4 cups of shredded zucchini
½ cup of shredded mozzarella
½ teaspoon of salt
4 tablespoons of grated
Parmesan cheese
½ teaspoon of salt
Ground black pepper as required
Grilled cheese
For Grilled Cheese:
1 tablespoon of butter melted in
room temperature
1/3 cup of freshly grated sharp
cheddar cheese at room
temperature

GRILLED CHEESE WITH A CRISPY ZUCCHINI CRUST

DIRECTIONS

1. For the zucchini crust "bread" slices, you first need to preheat the oven to 450°F. Place one rack in the middle.
2. Now take a baking sheet, line it with parchment paper, and grease it well. Or you can simply use a silicone baking mat.
3. In a microwave-safe dish, put all the shredded zucchini and microwave in high temperature for 6 minutes.
4. Transfer the zucchini to a tea towel or dishcloth and squeeze out the extra moisture. The zucchini has to be absolutely dry; otherwise, the dough will be mushy which you cannot slice as bread.

5. In a large bowl, mix the zucchini, mozzarella cheese, egg, Parmesan cheese, salt, oregano, and pepper. Spread the zucchini mixture on the lined baking sheet and create 4 squares.

6. Bake the squares for 15–20 minutes until everything is golden brown.
7. Remove them from oven and allow them to cool for 10 minutes before you peel them off from the parchment paper. Do not break them.
8. Now it is time to assemble the grilled cheese.
9. Take a pan and heat it over medium heat.
10. Butter each side, preferably the top of the zucchini bread crust.
11. Put one slice of bread in the pan, putting the buttered side down; sprinkle it with cheese and top it with the remaining zucchini crust bread with the buttered side at the top.
12. Turn down the heat and cook the bread slice until they are golden brown. This will take about 2–4 minutes.
13. Gently flip the bread slice and cook both the sides until they are golden brown.
14. Enjoy the warm and crispy, absolutely healthy zucchini bread slice.

Recipe Notes

MEXICAN MEATZA

MEXICAN MEATZA IN MINI SIZE

GENERAL INFO

Serving Size: 1
Servings Per Recipe: 4
Calories: 1,079
Preparation Time: 10 Minutes
Cooking Time: 25 Minutes

INGREDIENTS

1 pound of lean ground beef
1 egg
2 teaspoons of chili powder
½ onion
1 cup of riced cauliflower
1 teaspoon of cumin
½ teaspoon of pepper
1 teaspoon of salt
¼ thinly sliced red onion
1 teaspoon of garlic powder
1 cup of shredded cheddar cheese
¼ cup of sweet pepper slices
½ cup of sour cream
1 clove of garlic
1/3 cup of loosely packed cilantro leaves
1 tablespoon of freshly squeezed lime juice

NUTRITION INFO

Fat—82 g
Carbohydrate—6 g
Protein—77 g

MEXICAN MEATZA IN MINI SIZE

DIRECTIONS

1. Preheat the oven to 350°F.
2. Add onion to a food processor and wait until they are finely chopped.
3. Add the cauliflower to the food processor and wait until they look like grains of rice.
4. Add the onion and cauliflower along with meat, chili powder, beaten egg, salt, pepper, cumin powder, and garlic powder.
5. Mix them well and split the entire mixture into 4 portions.
6. Take one piece and create a very thin, round pizza shell. Repeat the process with other 3 portions. Place them on a sprayed cooking sheet. You may need 2 cooking sheets for the meat.
7. Bake the meat for 20 minutes; the meat should be thoroughly cooked. Remember that the thickness of the meat will determine the cooking time, but do not overcook the meat.
8. Take it out of the oven, sprinkle the cheese and add the pepper and onions on top of it.
9. Broil the meat for about 3 minutes until the cheese is melted.
10. Add the avocado pieces on the meatza and enjoy a slice.
11. You can also add some of your favorite toppings such as black olives, lettuce, tomatoes, sour cream, hot sauce, or onions.

Recipe Notes

PORK
CHOPS

PORK CHOPS WITH MOCK APPLES

GENERAL INFO

Serving Size: 1
Servings Per Recipe: 4
Calories: 288
Preparation Time: 5 Minutes
Cooking Time: 40 Minutes

INGREDIENTS

½ cup of lemon juice
½ teaspoon of sea salt
2 tablespoons of ghee
2 freshly chopped chayote into ½-inch chunks
4 boneless pork chops
1 teaspoon of cinnamon
2 tablespoons of monk fruit sweetener or any low-carb sweetener
1 tablespoon of apple cider vinegar
1/8 teaspoon of nutmeg

NUTRITION INFO

Carbohydrate—4.85 g
Fat—16 g
Sodium—356 mg
Cholesterol—108 mg
Protein—29 g
Potassium—582 mg

PORK CHOPS WITH MOCK APPLES

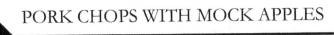

DIRECTIONS

1. Put a large skillet on medium heat and melt the ghee; add the pork chops and cook them for 5 minutes.

2. Now you need to flip the pork chops and add the chayote, cinnamon; sprinkle the sweetener, apple cider vinegar, and nutmeg on the top. Cook them for another 4–5 minutes until the pork chops are cooked as rare or medium rare. For medium rare, the temperature should reach 145°F, and for rare, it should reach 160°F.

3. Now you can remove the pork chops and put them in a meal prep container in case you are preparing meals for the entire week. If not, keep the pork chops warm until you need to serve them.

4. Now you can bring the chayote mixture to boil for quite a few minutes. Reduce the heat to low medium and simmer the concoction by covering it. Allow it to simmer for 30–40 minutes, but do not forget to stir occasionally.

5. You will know that the chayote is ready when it is so tender that you can pierce them with a fork. The texture will be similar toa baked apple.

6. Serve the chayote mock apples with pork and enjoy a delicious meal.

Recipe Notes

SESAME SALMON

SESAME SALMON

GENERAL INFO

Serving Size: 4
Servings Per Recipe: 1
Calories: 449
Preparation Time: 60 Minutes
Cooking Time: 20 Minutes

NUTRITION INFO

Fat—12 g
Protein—18 g
Carbohydrate—6.1 g

INGREDIENTS

2 Portobello mushroom caps or baby bella mushrooms
4–6 ounces of salmon fillet
1 tablespoon of toasted sesame seeds
1 baby bok choy
1 green onion
1 teaspoon of sesame oil
½ freshly squeezed lemon juice
1 teaspoon of olive oil
1 tablespoon of coconut aminos
½ teaspoon of salt
½ inch of freshly grated ginger
½ teaspoon of black pepper

SESAME SALMON

DIRECTIONS

1. Take all the ingredients of marinade like sesame oil, olive oil, coconut aminos, ginger, lemon juice, salt, and pepper and whisk them.
2. On one half of the salmon fillet, drizzle some of the marinade. Turn the fillet and coat it with marinade on the other side. Cover the salmon and refrigerate it for an hour.
3. Now preheat the oven to 400°F.
4. Now trim the rough ends from the bok choy and cut them into halves. The mushrooms should be sliced into ½-inch pieces.
5. Now take the rest of the marinade and drizzle it over the veggies. Put the vegetables on a lined baking sheet.
6. Put the salmon with its skin down on the lined baking sheet along with the veggies. Bake till the salmon is cooked; it will take about 20 minutes for the salmon to cook.
7. Top the salmon with sliced green onions and sesame seeds.
8. Enjoy a hearty meal with your loved one.

Recipe Notes

STUFFED TOMATOES

STUFFED TOMATOES

GENERAL INFO

Serving Size: 1
Servings Per Recipe: 1
Calories: 196
Preparation Time: 5 Minutes
Cooking Time: 10 Minutes

INGREDIENTS

1 can of well-drained tuna
1 medium-size tomato
2 teaspoons of balsamic vinegar
1 tablespoon of chopped fresh basil
1 tablespoon of chopped mozzarella
1 tablespoon of chopped green onion

NUTRITION INFO

Fat—12 g
Fat—5.9 g
Sodium—400.4 mg
Cholesterol—33.8 g
Carbohydrate—10.7 g
Potassium—389.2 mg
Protein—14.5 g

STUFFED TOMATOES

DIRECTIONS

1. Cut ¼ inch off from the top of the tomato. Use a spoon to scoop the insides of the tomato. Keep it aside while you prepare the tuna salad.
2. Take a large bowl and stir the drained tuna, mozzarella, balsamic vinegar, green onion, and basil. Put the tuna salad inside the hollow tomato and enjoy the stuffed tomatoes.
3. You would love this easy-to-make simple recipe, which can be enjoyed at your leisure.

Recipe Notes

TURKEY SAUSAGE FRITTATA

TURKEY SAUSAGE FRITTATA

GENERAL INFO

Serving Size: 1
Servings Per Recipe: 8
Calories: 240
Preparation Time: 10 Minutes
Cooking Time: 30 Minutes

INGREDIENTS

2 bell peppers
12 ounces of ground breakfast sausage turkey
12 cups of sour cream without lactose
1 teaspoon of black pepper
1 teaspoon of Himalayan pink salt
2 ounces of shredded Tillamook cheddar
12 eggs
2 teaspoons of Kerry gold butter

NUTRITION INFO

Protein—16.7 g
Carbohydrate—5.5 g
Fat—16.7 g

TURKEY SAUSAGE FRITTATA

DIRECTIONS

1. First, you need to preheat the oven to 350°F.
2. In a blender, crack all the eggs; add the black pepper, salt, and sour cream; and blend for 30 seconds in high mode. Keep this mixture aside.
3. Take a large skillet and put it on the stove at medium heat. Add the butter.
4. Slice the bell peppers into strips and add it to the butter. Sauté them until they turn brown; let them be tender as well. It will take about 6 minutes. Take out the peppers from the skillet.
5. In the same butter, add the turkey sausage and keep on stirring them till the meat is brown. It will take about 8 minutes. Now flatten the turkey at the bottom and layer it with pepper and put the egg mix on top of everything.
6. Put the skillet in the oven and set the baking mode for 30 minutes. If you want some extra creaminess, you can add the cheese after you take out the frittata from the oven. The cheese will melt and create a lovely golden topping.

DINNER
RECIPES

BROCCOLI AND BEEF BOWLS

BROCCOLI AND BEEF BOWLS

GENERAL INFO

Serving Size: 1
Servings Per Recipe: 4
Calories: 370
Preparation Time: 10 Minutes
Cooking Time: 30 Minutes

NUTRITION INFO

Fat—9 g
Sodium—950 mg
Cholesterol—10 mg
Protein—21 g
Carbohydrate—5 g

INGREDIENTS

1 pound of grass-fed 85% lean beef
1 tablespoon of cooking fat
1 teaspoon of granulated garlic
1 teaspoon of fine salt
1 tablespoon of coconut aminos
1 tablespoon of avocado oil
4 broccoli crowns shaped into florets
½ teaspoon of fine salt
2 tablespoons of sunflower seed butter
1 tablespoon of cooking fat
½ cup of bone broth
A pinch of fine salt
1 teaspoon of ground ginger
Freshly squeezed lemon juice
1 finely minced green onion
1 teaspoon of coconut aminos
4 cups of baby spinach

BROCCOLI AND BEEF BOWLS

DIRECTIONS

1. First, you need to preheat the oven to 400°F.
2. Toss the broccoli in fat and salt on a sheet pan. Massage the florets and spread them evenly on the sheet without overcrowding them.
3. As the ovenpreheats, put the sheet, and once the oven stops at the designated temperature, set the time for 20 minutes.
4. On medium heat, put a large skillet and add the remaining fat. Put the beef into the skillet, crumble it, and add garlic and salt. Keep on stirring it till they are brown and have crumbled properly. Add the coconut aminos and bring the temperature to high.
5. Cook the beef until they are brown, and keep on stirring them occasionally. The beef should be crispy.

6. While the beef is cooked, put a small sauce pot on medium heat.
7. Melt the fat and the sunflower seed butter. Keep on stirring them until it is smooth.
8. Keep on adding the bone broth, aminos, ground ginger, and salt, and keep on stirring them until they are combined. Put everything on simmer.
9. Put the lemon juice and stir everything until it is light and smooth.
10. Keep on adding the bone broth, aminos, ground ginger, and salt, and keep on stirring them until they are combined. Put everything on simmer.
11. Put the lemon juice and stir everything until it is light and smooth.
12. Now add the green onion and remove the sauce from the heat.
13. In 4 large bowls, create a bed of baby spinach, and put ground beef in each bowls. Add the broccoli florets and layer it with the sauce. It is time to dig into these delightful delights.

Recipe Notes

PORK FRIED RICE

PORK FRIED RICE

GENERAL INFO

Serving Size: 1
Servings Per Recipe: 4–5
Calories: 399
Preparation Time: 15 Minutes
Cooking Time: 30 Minutes

INGREDIENTS

2 large eggs
2 freshly chopped cloves of garlic
½ head of medium cauliflower
100 grams of pork belly
2 spring onions
1 teaspoon of black sesame seeds
2 small green capsicums
1 tablespoon of soy sauce
1 teaspoon of pickled ginger

NUTRITION INFO

Carbohydrate—12 g
Fat—32 g
Protein—16 g

PORK FRIED RICE

DIRECTIONS

1. First, you need chop the cauliflower into florets
2. Put the cauliflower into a food processor and blend it until it forms rice-sized granules. Be careful with the florets, so that they do not turn into a mash.
3. In a wok or a frying pan, heat some oil, add the cauliflower, and sauté them for 5 minutes in medium heat. Keep them aside after they are cooked.
4. Beat the eggs and put them in a frying pan. Swirl the mixture so that you have a thin omelet. After it is cooked, flip it and cook for another minute. Put it aside for later use.
5. In the same oil, add the garlic and keep frying it till it is fragrant. Now add the pork belly. While the pork is cooked, slice the omelet into small cubes.
6. Once the pork belly is cooked, add the capsicum, half of the spring onion, and cook for another minute.
7. Now you should add the cauliflower and eggs in the frying pan. Add the soy sauce and keep on stirring the mixture.
8. Cook everything in high heat till all the ingredients are well combined. Serve the rice hot.
9. You can garnish the rice with remaining spring onions, sesame seeds,and pickled ginger. Serve this oriental delight to your guests with your favorite side dish.

Recipe Notes

SALMON GREMOLATA

SALMON GREMOLATA WITH ROASTED VEGGIES

GENERAL INFO

Serving Size: 1
Servings Per Recipe: 4
Calories: 494
Preparation Time: 10 Minutes
Cooking Time: 20 Minutes

INGREDIENTS

2 cloves of garlic
4 salmon fillets
Lemon zest
1 tablespoon of olive oil
1 cup of almond flour
Pepper
Salt
1 cup of cherry tomatoes
1 bunch of asparagus
1 tablespoon of olive oil
¼ cup of parsley leaves

NUTRITION INFO

Fat—31 g
Sodium—83 mg
Carbohydrate—12 g
Cholesterol—93 mg
Potassium—1,162 mg
Protein—42 g

SALMON GREMOLATA WITH ROASTED VEGGIES

DIRECTIONS

1. Heat your oven to 350°F for a fan oven and 380°F for a non-fan oven.
2. In a food processor or blender, blitz the garlic, almond, and parsley, and then, add the lemon zest.
3. On a parchment lined or greased sheet, put the salmon fillets. Season them with pepper and salt, and spray a little oil. Now put the gremolata crumb mixture on top of the salmon fillets.
4. If you want to roast the veggies with salmon, toss them in little oil, put them around salmon on the sheet pan, and add salt and pepper to it.
5. Bake everything for 15–20 minutes until the fish is cooked and the top becomes golden.

Recipe Notes

TUNA FISH SALAD

TUNA FISH SALAD

GENERAL INFO

Serving Size: 1
Servings Per Recipe: 4–5
Calories: 563
Preparation Time: 10 Minutes
Cooking Time: 10 Minutes

NUTRITION INFO

Fat—30.9 g
Cholesterol—70 mg
Carbohydrate—37.5 g
Protein—41.8 g
Sodium—1,579 mg

INGREDIENTS

1 freshly diced large tomato
¼ cup of freshly chopped mint leaves
2 cups of mixed greens
¼ cup of freshly chopped parsley leaves
1 lengthwise sliced small zucchini
10 large pitted Kalamata olives
½ freshly diced avocado
1 freshly sliced green onion
1 tablespoon of extra-virgin olive oil
1 can of drained chunk of light tuna
1 tablespoon of balsamic vinegar
½ teaspoon of freshly cracked black pepper
¼ teaspoon of fine sea or Himalayan sea salt

TUNA FISH SALAD

DIRECTIONS

1. Grill the zucchini slices on both the sides in a sizzling hot cast iron skillet grill pan. The other option is to use an extremely hot grill.
2. Remove the pan from heat and allow it to cool for a few minutes. Cut the zucchini into bite size pieces.
3. In a large mixing bowl, combine all the ingredients and stir them delicately.
4. Serve the fresh salad and enjoy a healthy meal.

Recipe Notes

TUSCAN GARLIC CHICKEN

TUSCAN GARLIC CHICKEN

GENERAL INFO

Serving Size: 1
Servings Per Recipe: 4–6
Calories: 322
Preparation Time: 10 Minutes
Cooking Time: 15 Minutes

INGREDIENTS

2 tablespoons of olive oil
½ cup of chicken broth
1 ½ pounds of thinly sliced skinless boneless chicken breasts
1 cup of heavy cream
1 teaspoon of Italian seasoning
1 cup of freshly chopped spinach
1 teaspoon of garlic powder
½ cup of Parmesan cheese
½ cup of sun-dried tomatoes

NUTRITION INFO

Fat—19 g
Carbohydrate—4 g
Protein—33 g

TUSCAN GARLIC CHICKEN

DIRECTIONS

1. Take a large skillet, add the olive oil, and start by cooking the chicken on medium-high heat for about 5 minutes. Cook the chicken in such a way, so that both the sides are evenly browned. You will know that the chicken is ready when it is no longer pink in the center.
2. Keep the chicken on a plate for later use.
3. Now in the skillet, add the chicken broth, heavy cream, Italian seasoning, garlic powder, and Parmesan cheese. Whisk all the ingredients on medium-high heat till the sauce start to thicken.
4. Now add the tomatoes and the spinach and let everything simmer; after a few minutes, you will notice that the spinach has started to wilt. Now add the chicken to the pan.
5. Prepare the dish in a jiffy, if you are not in a mood to cook an elaborate meal.

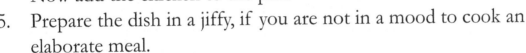

Recipe Notes

VEGAN CURRY A LA THAI STYLE

VEGAN CURRY A LA THAI STYLE

GENERAL INFO

Serving Size: 1
Servings Per Recipe: 4
Calories: 318
Preparation Time: 5 Minutes
Cooking Time: 15 Minutes

INGREDIENTS

2 tablespoons of coconut oil

1 tofu pack: 454 grams cut into 16 cubes

2 red and green bell peppers cut into strips

1 tablespoon of tomato paste

2 teaspoons of chili flakes

15 ounces of canned coconut milk with full fat

1 tablespoon of almond butter

1 teaspoon of Thai curry paste

1 stalk of lemongrass cut into 3 pieces

1 thumb-sized ginger neatly peeled

¼ cup of soy sauce

1 clove of garlic

1 tablespoon of tomato paste

NUTRITION INFO

Fat—27.1 g
Carbohydrate—9.1 g
Protein—12 g
Sodium—961 mg
Potassium—350 mg

VEGAN CURRY A LA THAI STYLE

DIRECTIONS

1. At medium heat, heat a pan and melt the coconut oil. Now you need to mince the garlic and ginger and add them to the pan.

2. Now you need to add the bell pepper strips and lemongrass. Stir them for 30 seconds and add the chili flakes with coconut milk. Keep on stirring.

3. Into that mixture, add the soy sauce, tomato, Thai curry paste, and almond butter. Stir everything for 1 minute and add the tofu cubes. The curry should be cooked for 5–10 minutes. When the sauce thickens, take it off from the heat.

4. Serve the delicious vegan curry with chopped green onions and coriander, which will add some freshness to the dish.

NOTES

THANK YOU

Made in the USA
Middletown, DE
29 January 2019